Properties of Materials

Hard or Soft

Charlotte Guillain

Heinemann Library
Chicago, Illinois

www.heinemannraintree.com
Visit our website to find out more information about Heinemann-Raintree books.

To order:

☎ Phone 888-454-2279

💻 Visit www.heinemannraintree.com to browse our catalog and order online.

Designed by Joanna Hinton-Malivoire
Photo research by Elizabeth Alexander
Printed and bound by South China Printing Company Ltd

13 12 11 10 09
10 9 8 7 6 5 4 3 2 1

Library of Congress Cataloging-in-Publication Data
Guillain, Charlotte.
  Hard or soft / Charlotte Guillain.
    p. cm. -- (Properties of materials)
  Includes bibliographical references and index.
  ISBN 978-1-4329-3270-1 (hc) -- ISBN 978-1-4329-3293-0
(pb) 1. Hardness--Juvenile literature. 2. Hard materials--
Juvenile literature. I. Title.
  TA418.42G85 2008
  620.1'126--dc22
                              2008055118

Acknowledgments
The author and publishers are grateful to the following for permission to reproduce copyright material: Alamy pp. **6** (© Geoff du Feu), **10** (© Dirk V. Mallinckrodt); © Capstone Publishers pp. **8**, **19**, **22** (Karon Dubke); © Corbis p. **15**; Corbis pp. **20** (© Image Source), **21**, **23** middle (© Graham Bell); Getty Images p. **14** (Somos/Veer); Photolibrary pp. **13** (Stockdisc/Stockbyte), **18** (Imagesource); Shutterstock pp. **4** (© Gilmanshin), **5** (© Ilja Mašík), **7** (© Leonid Katsyka), **9** (© Mindy W. M. Chung), **11**, **23** bottom (© GoodMood Photo), **12**, **23** top (© Olivier Le Queinec), **16** (© PhotoSky.4t.com), **17** (© IKO).

Cover photograph of the Devil's Marbles reproduced with permission of © Dorling Kindersley (Alan Keohane). Back cover photograph of a girl knocking on a door reproduced with permission of Photolibrary (Imagesource).

The publishers would like to thank Nancy Harris and Adriana Scalise for their assistance in the preparation of this book.

Every effort has been made to contact copyright holders of any material reproduced in this book. Any omissions will be rectified in subsequent printings if notice is given to the publisher.

Contents

Hard Materials

Some things are hard.

It is not easy to change the shape of hard things.

Hard things can be heavy.

Hard things can be strong.

Soft Materials

Some things are soft.

It is easy to change the shape of soft things.

Soft things can be light.

Soft things can be stretchy.

Hard and Soft Materials

Metal is hard.

Metal can be strong.

Wool is soft.

Wool can be stretchy.

Glass is hard.

Glass can be heavy.

Cotton is soft.

Cotton can be light.

Rock is hard. It is not easy to change the shape of rock.

Clay is soft. It is easy to change the shape of wet clay.

You can feel if something is hard.

You can feel if something is soft.

Hard things are not easy to squeeze.

Soft things are easy to squeeze.

Quiz

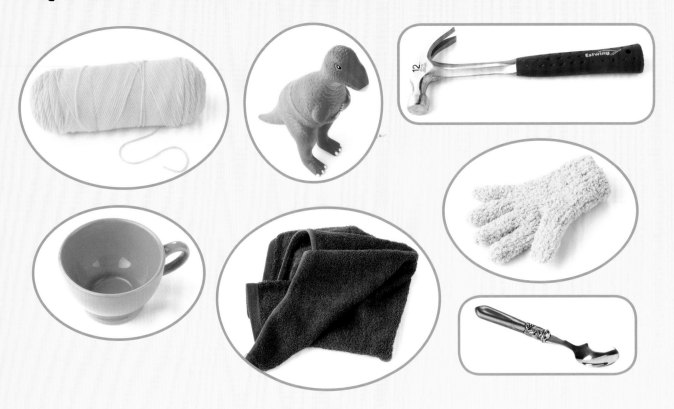

Which of these things are hard?

Which of these things are soft?

Picture Glossary

 **metal** hard, shiny material

 **squeeze** press something tightly

 **stretchy** able to become longer or wider when pulled

Index

Note to Parents and Teachers

Before Reading

Tell children materials can be hard or soft. Materials that are hard can be heavy and cannot change shape easily. Materials that are soft can be light, easy to squeeze, and can change shape easily. Hold up different pictures of soft and hard materials. Ask children to describe the pictures. Are the objects hard or soft?

After Reading

Discuss with children the different types of materials they saw in the book. Ask children what they noticed about the hard and soft materials? If they were to build a house, what materials would they want their house to be made out of? Read a traditional version of *The Three Little Pigs*, and have children think about what type of material built the strongest house for the pigs. After reading, have children work in small groups to investigate various building materials (e.g., styrofoam, toothpicks, clay, blocks, paper, and cardboard). Tell children to divide their materials into two groups: hard and soft. Ask them which group is better to build a house and why. After the discussion, let children work in groups to build their own houses, then discuss which ones are the strongest.